DESIGNS FROM PRE-COLUMBIAN MEXICO

DESIGNS FROM PRE-COLUMBIAN MEXICO

Jorge Enciso

Dover Publications, Inc.

NEW YORK

Designs from Pre-Columbian Mexico is a new work, first published by Dover Publications, Inc., in 1971.

DOVER *Pictorial Archive* SERIES

International Standard Book Number: 0-486-22794-4
Library of Congress Catalog Card Number: 73-168905

Manufactured in the United States of America
Dover Publications, Inc.
180 Varick Street
New York, N.Y. 10014

To the Memory of
Jorge Enciso
1880–1969

PUBLISHER'S NOTE

Jorge Enciso, born in the state of Jalisco, was an outstanding figure in the bustling cultural and political life of Mexico City in the post-Revolution 1920's.

Devoting himself at first to caricature and painting—he was one of the pioneers of the "Mural Renaissance"—he soon earned a lasting reputation as a historian and protector of Mexico's Pre-Columbian and Colonial art treasures, an important collector in his own right, and one of the beautifiers of modern Mexico City.

Enciso helped arrange the folk art display at Mexico's Centennial Exhibition in 1921. He became Custodian of Colonial Monuments, Assistant Director of the National Institute of Anthropology and History, and member of the Mexican Association of Art Critics.

His earlier book "Design Motifs of Ancient Mexico (Sellos del Antiguo México)" is considered to be a classic of scholarship and illustration. Enciso himself made the selection and did all the renderings of the designs in the present book, which is here published for the first time anywhere.

All the designs in this book are from the surfaces of "malacates," spindle whorls like the one illustrated in the Mexican pictorial manuscript called the Codex Vindobonensis (see figure). These objects of baked clay, in the form of small receptacles, are circular in section and have a circular hole through their center. "Malacates," which vary somewhat in size, are found in the oldest Mexican archeological digs, and were very common just before the Conquest. Some were modeled by hand, some mass-produced in molds. Many were covered with luster slips and decorated with stamped or incised designs, either abstract or representing people, animals and plants.

Mr. Enciso selected these designs from "malacates" (from sites throughout Mexico) in the Museo Nacional de Antropología in Mexico City, the Museo Arqueológico in Teotihuacán and the Museo Regional de Antropología e Historia in Tuxtla Gutiérrez (Chiapas). He also included designs from "malacates" in the private collections of Diego Rivera, Roberto Montenegro, Angel Rodríguez, William Spratling, Agustín Gómez y Gutiérrez, Dr. Artemio Jácome, Eduardo Mead, Jorge Hauswaldt, Helmuth Franck, Kurt Schleu, B. Meneses, Raúl Dehesa, Demetrio García, Guillermo Echaniz and others.

The captions in this book give Mr. Enciso's identifications of the motifs on the "malacates."

DESIGNS FROM PRE-COLUMBIAN MEXICO

The monkey (Ocomatli). 1

2   (1) Heron (Astatl). (2) Quetzal (Quetzalli).

(1) Eagle (Cuauhtli). (2) Vultures. (3) Kingfisher (?).   **3**

4   (1) Roadrunner or chachalaca. (2) and (3) Flowers.

Variants of the Xicalcoliuhqui fret motif.   **5**

6   Variants of the Xicalcoliuhqui fret motif.

The eagle (Cuauhtli).   **7**

8 The eagle (Cuauhtli).

The eagle (Cuauhtli).   **9**

10   Angular and curvilinear spirals.

Angular and curvilinear spirals.   11

12   (1) Spiral design. (2) Flower.

Unspecified geometrical motifs: circles, hooks, angular
spirals and elements of the Xicalcoliuhqui fret.   **13**

Quetzals, nos. (1) and (3) with special reference to
the feathered serpent Quetzalcóatl.

(1) and (2) Quetzals. (3) Head of a chachalaca. **15**

16　The buzzard (Cascacuauhtli).

The buzzard (Cascacuauhtli). **17**

18   Unidentified flowers.

Unidentified flowers.

22   Unidentified fantastic animals.

Unidentified fantastic animals.   23

24   Unidentified flowers.

Unspecified geometrical motifs: circles, lines, etc.

Unspecified geometrical motifs: circles, lines, etc.

Human figures. **27**

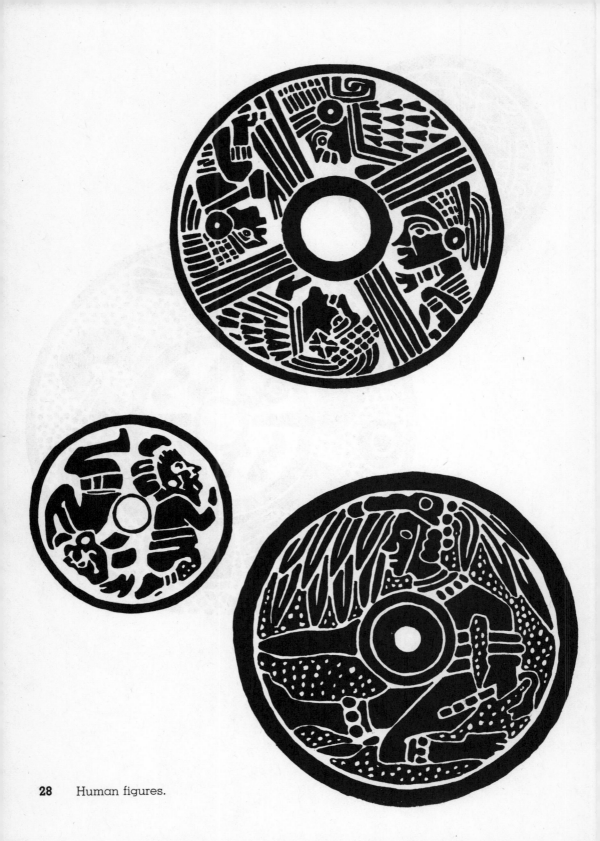

28 Human figures.

Human figures.

30   The dog (Itzcuintli).

The dog (Itzcuintli).

(1) The jaguar (Ocelotl).

(2) and (3) Heads of pumas (Mixtli).

Unidentified flowers.   33

Unidentified flowers.

Unspecified geometrical motifs, predominantly
circles, hooks and Xicalcoliuhqui frets. **35**

Unspecified geometrical motifs, predominantly
circles, hooks and Xicalcoliuhqui frets.

Unidentified birds. **37**

38   Unidentified birds.

Unidentified birds. **39**

40   Various geometrical motifs, apparently of great antiquity.

Various geometrical motifs, apparently of great antiquity. **41**

　Unidentified animals.

Unidentified animals.

44   The dog (Itzcuintli).

(1) and (3) The dog (Itzcuintli). (2) The "old coyote" (Ueuecoyotl). **45**

46   The monkey (Ocomatli).

The monkey (Ocomatli). **47**

48   Ritual masks.

50   Human figures.

Unidentified flowers.

52 Unidentified flowers.

Unidentified flowers.

54   Unidentified flowers.

Unidentified flowers. **55**

Unidentified flowers.

Unidentified flowers.   **57**

58 Unidentified flowers.

Unidentified flowers.   **59**

Unspecified geometrical motifs, predominantly circles, parallel lines, tri-
angles, squares, crosses and broken
lines.

Unspecified geometrical motifs, predominantly circles, parallel lines, tri-
angles, squares, crosses and broken
lines. **61**

Hooks, angular spirals and elements of the Xicalcoliuhqui fret.

Hooks, angular spirals and elements of the Xicalcoliuhqui fret.   **63**

64 Variants of the Xicalcoliuhqui fret and circular motifs.

Variants of the Xicalcoliuhqui fret and circular motifs.

66 Variants of the Xicalcoliuhqui fret.

Variants of the Xicalcoliuhqui fret. **67**

Unidentified flowers.

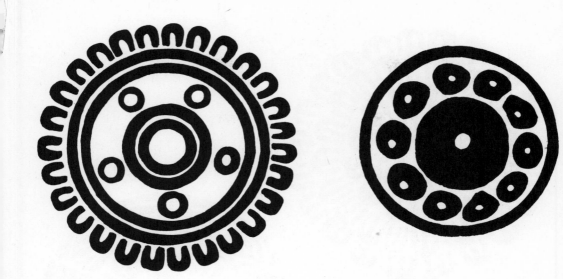

Unidentified flowers. **69**

70   Unidentified flowers.

Unspecified geometrical motifs. **73**

74 Unspecified geometrical motifs.

Variants of the fire serpent (Xiuhcouatl). **75**

76   Variants of the fire serpent (Xiuhcouatl).

Variants of the fire serpent (Xiuhcouatl).

78 Unspecified geometrical motifs.

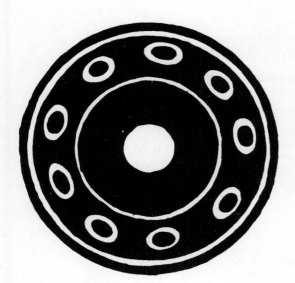

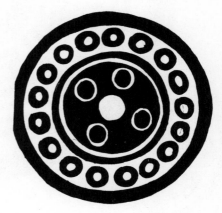

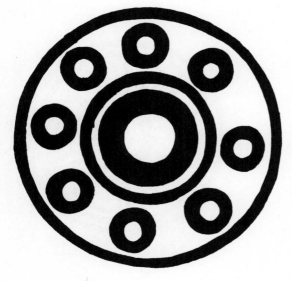

Unspecified geometrical motifs.   **79**

80   Hooks, angular spirals and elements of the Xicalcoliuhqui fret.

Variants of the Xicalcoliuhqui fret.   **81**

82   Hooks, angular spirals and elements of the Xicalcoliuhqui fret.

Hooks, angular spirals and elements of the Xicalcoliuhqui fret.

84   Hooks, angular spirals and elements of the Xicalcoliuhqui fret.

Unspecified geometrical motifs, predominantly circles, hooks and dots.

86   Unspecified geometrical motifs, predominantly circles, hooks and dots.

Unspecified geometrical motifs, predominantly circles, hooks and dots.

88   Various geometrical motifs composed of lines, hooks and balanced masses.

Variant of the Xicalcoliuhqui fret. **89**

90   Variant of the Xicalcoliuhqui fret.

Stepped motifs and the Xicalcoliuhqui fret. **91**

92   Stepped motif.

Unspecified geometrical motifs.   **93**

94   Unspecified geometrical motifs.

Unspecified geometrical motif.   95

96 Unspecified geometrical motifs.

Unspecified geometrical motifs.   **97**

98   Geometrical motif with variations of lines and dots.

Geometrical motifs with variations of lines and dots.   **99**

100 Geometrical motifs with variations of lines and dots.

Variants of the blue worm sign (Xonecuilli). **101**

102 Variants of the blue worm sign (Xonecuilli).

Variants of the blue worm sign (Xonecuilli). **103**

104 Unidentified flowers.

Dover Books on Art

Dover Books on Art

MASTERPIECES OF FURNITURE, Verna Cook Salomonsky. Photographs and measured drawings of some of the finest examples of Colonial American, 17th century English, Windsor, Sheraton, Hepplewhite, Chippendale, Louis XIV, Queen Anne, and various other furniture styles. The textual matter includes information on traditions, characteristics, background, etc. of various pieces. 101 plates. Bibliography. 224pp. 7⅞ x 10¾.

21381-1 Paperbound $2.50

PRIMITIVE ART, Franz Boas. In this exhaustive volume, a great American anthropologist analyzes all the fundamental traits of primitive art, covering the formal element in art, representative art, symbolism, style, literature, music, and the dance. Illustrations of Indian embroidery, paleolithic paintings, woven blankets, wing and tail designs, totem poles, cutlery, earthenware, baskets and many other primitive objects and motifs. Over 900 illustrations. 376pp. 5⅜ x 8.

20025-6 Paperbound $2.50

AN INTRODUCTION TO A HISTORY OF WOODCUT, A. M. Hind. Nearly all of this authoritative 2-volume set is devoted to the 15th century—the period during which the woodcut came of age as an important art form. It is the most complete compendium of information on this period, the artists who contributed to it, and their technical and artistic accomplishments. Profusely illustrated with cuts by 15th century masters, and later works for comparative purposes. 484 illustrations. 5 indexes. Total of xi + 838pp. 5⅜ x 8½. Two-vols. 20952-0, 20953-9 Paperbound $5.50

ART STUDENTS' ANATOMY, E. J. Farris. Teaching anatomy by using chiefly living objects for illustration, this study has enjoyed long popularity and success in art courses and home-study programs. All the basic elements of the human anatomy are illustrated in minute detail, diagrammed and pictured as they pass through common movements and actions. 158 drawings, photographs, and roentgenograms. Glossary of anatomical terms. x + 159pp. 5⅝ x 8⅜.

20744-7 Paperbound $1.50

COLONIAL LIGHTING, A. H. Hayward. The only book to cover the fascinating story of lamps and other lighting devices in America. Beginning with rush light holders used by the early settlers, it ranges through the elaborate chandeliers of the Federal period. illustrating 647 lamps. Of great value to antique collectors, designers, and historians of arts and crafts. Revised and enlarged by James R. Marsh. xxxi + 198pp. 5⅝ x 8¼.

20975-X Paperbound $2.00

AFRICAN SCULPTURE, Ladislas Segy. 163 full-page plates illustrating masks, fertility figures, ceremonial objects, etc., of 50 West and Central African tribes—95% never before illustrated. 34-page introduction to African sculpture. "Mr. Segy is one of its top authorities," NEW YORKER. 164 full-page photographic plates. Introduction. Bibliography. 244pp. 6⅛ x 9¼.

20396-4 Paperbound $2.25

CALLIGRAPHY, J. G. Schwandner. First reprinting in 200 years of this legendary book of beautiful handwriting. Over 300 ornamental initials, 12 complete calligraphic alphabets, over 150 ornate frames and panels, 75 calligraphic pictures of cherubs, stags, lions, etc., thousands of flourishes, scrolls, etc., by the greatest 18th-century masters. All material can be copied or adapted without permission. Historical introduction. 158 full-page plates. 368pp. 9 x 13.

20475-8 Clothbound $10.00

A DIDEROT PICTORIAL ENCYCLOPEDIA OF TRADES AND INDUSTRY. Manufacturing and the Technical Arts in Plates Selected from "L'Encyclopédie ou Dictionnaire Raisonné des Sciences, des Arts, et des Métiers," of Denis Diderot, edited with text by C. Gillispie. Over 2000 illustrations on 485 full-page plates. Magnificent 18th-century engravings of men, women, and children working at such trades as milling flour, cheesemaking, charcoal burning, mining, silverplating, shoeing horses, making fine glass, printing, hundreds more, showing details of machinery, different steps in sequence, etc. A remarkable art work, but also the largest collection of working figures in print, copyright-free, for art directors, designers, etc. Two vols. 920pp. 9 x 12. Heavy library cloth.

22284-5, 22285-3 Two volume set $22.50

SILK SCREEN TECHNIQUES, J. Biegeleisen, M. Cohn. A practical step-by-step home course in one of the most versatile, least expensive graphic arts processes. How to build an inexpensive silk screen, prepare stencils, print, achieve special textures, use color, etc. Every step explained, diagrammed. 149 illustrations, 201pp. 6⅛ x 9¼.

20433-2 Paperbound $2.00

STICKS AND STONES, Lewis Mumford. An examination of forces influencing American architecture: the medieval tradition in early New England, the classical influence in Jefferson's time, the Brown Decades, the imperial facade, the machine age, etc. "A truly remarkable book," SAT. REV. OF LITERATURE. 2nd revised edition. 21 illus. xvii + 240pp. 5⅜ x 8.

20202-X Paperbound $2.00

ART ANATOMY, *Dr. William Rimmer.* One of the few books on art anatomy that are themselves works of art, this is a faithful reproduction (rearranged for handy use) of the extremely rare masterpiece of the famous 19th century anatomist, sculptor, and art teacher. Beautiful, clear line drawings show every part of the body—bony structure, muscles, features, etc. Unusual are the sections on falling bodies, foreshortenings, muscles in tension, grotesque personalities, and Rimmer's remarkable interpretation of emotions and personalities as expressed by facial features. It will supplement every other book on art anatomy you are likely to have. Reproduced clearer than the lithographic original (which sells for $500 on up on the rare book market.) Over 1,200 illustrations. xiii + 153pp. 7¾ x 10¾.

20908-3 Paperbound $2.50

THE CRAFTSMAN'S HANDBOOK, *Cennino Cennini.* The finest English translation of IL LIBRO DELL' ARTE, the 15th century introduction to art technique that is both a mirror of Quatrocento life and a source of many useful but nearly forgotten facets of the painter's art. 4 illustrations. xxvii + 142pp. D. V. Thompson, translator. 5⅜ x 8.   20054-X Paperbound $1.75

THE BROWN DECADES, *Lewis Mumford.* A picture of the "buried renaissance" of the post-Civil War period, and the founding of modern architecture (Sullivan, Richardson, Root, Roebling), landscape development (Marsh, Olmstead, Eliot), and the graphic arts (Homer, Eakins, Ryder). 2nd revised, enlarged edition. Bibliography. 12 illustrations. xiv + 266 pp. 5⅜ x 8.

20200-3 Paperbound $2.00

THE HUMAN FIGURE, *J. H. Vanderpoel.* Not just a picture book, but a complete course by a famous figure artist. Extensive text, illustrated by 430 pencil and charcoal drawings of both male and female anatomy. 2nd enlarged edition. Foreword. 430 illus. 143pp. 6⅛ x 9¼.   20432-4 Paperbound $1.50

PINE FURNITURE OF EARLY NEW ENGLAND, *R. H. Kettell.* Over 400 illustrations, over 50 working drawings of early New England chairs, benches, beds, cupboards, mirrors, shelves, tables, other furniture esteemed for simple beauty and character. "Rich store of illustrations . . . emphasizes the individuality and varied design," ANTIQUES. 413 illustrations, 55 working drawings. 475pp. 8 x 10¾.   20145-4 Clothbound $10.00

GREEK REVIVAL ARCHITECTURE IN AMERICA, T. Hamlin. A comprehensive study of the American Classical Revival, its regional variations, reasons for its success and eventual decline. Profusely illustrated with photos, sketches, floor plans and sections, displaying the work of almost every important architect of the time. 2 appendices. 39 figures, 94 plates containing 221 photos, 62 architectural designs, drawings, etc. 324-item classified bibliography. Index. xi + 439pp. 5⅜ x 8½.

21148-7 Paperbound $3.50

CREATIVE LITHOGRAPHY AND HOW TO DO IT, Grant Arnold. Written by a man who practiced and taught lithography for many years, this highly useful volume explains all the steps of the lithographic process from tracing the drawings on the stone to printing the lithograph, with helpful hints for solving special problems. Index. 16 reproductions of lithographs. 11 drawings. xv + 214pp. of text. 5⅜ x 8½.

21208-4 Paperbound $2.25

TEACH YOURSELF ANTIQUE COLLECTING, E. Bradford. An excellent, brief guide to collecting British furniture, silver, pictures and prints, pewter, pottery and porcelain, Victoriana, enamels, clocks or other antiques. Much background information difficult to find elsewhere. 15pp. of illus. 215pp. 7 x 4¼.

21368-4 Clothbound $2.00

THE STANDARD BOOK OF QUILT MAKING AND COLLECTING, M. Ickis. Even if you are a beginner, you will soon find yourself quilting like an expert, by following these clearly drawn patterns, photographs, and step-by-step instructions. Learn how to plan the quilt, to select the pattern to harmonize with the design and color of the room, to choose materials. Over 40 full-size patterns. Index. 483 illustrations. One color plate. xi + 276pp. 6¾ x 9½.   20582-7 Paperbound $2.50

THE ENJOYMENT AND USE OF COLOR, W. Sargent. Requiring no special technical know-how, this book tells you all about color and how it is created, perceived, and imitated in art. Covers many little-known facts about color values, intensities, effects of high and low illumination, complementary colors, and color harmonies. Simple do-it-yourself experiments and observations. 35 illustrations, including 6 full-page color plates. New color frontispiece. Index. x + 274 pp. 5⅜ x 8.

20944-X Paperbound $2.25

Dover Books on Art

LANDSCAPE GARDENING IN JAPAN, Josiah Conder. A detailed picture of Japanese gardening techniques and ideas, the artistic principles incorporated in the Japanese garden, and the religious and ethical concepts at the heart of those principles. Preface. 92 illustrations, plus all 40 full-page plates from the Supplement. Index. xv + 299pp. 8⅜ x 11¼.

21216-5 Paperbound $3.50

DESIGN AND FIGURE CARVING, E. J. Tangerman. "Anyone who can peel a potato can carve," states the author, and in this unusual book he shows you how, covering every stage in detail from very simple exercises working up to museum-quality pieces. Terrific aid for hobbyists, arts and crafts counselors, teachers, those who wish to make reproductions for the commercial market. Appendix: How to Enlarge a Design. Brief bibliography. Index. 1298 figures. x + 289pp. 5⅜ x 8½.

21209-2 Paperbound $2.00

WILD FOWL DECOYS, Joel Barber. Antique dealers, collectors, craftsmen, hunters, readers of Americana, etc. will find this the only thorough and reliable guide on the market today to this unique folk art. It contains the history, cultural significance, regional design variations; unusual decoy lore; working plans for constructing decoys; and loads of illustrations. 140 full-page plates, 4 in color. 14 additional plates of drawings and plans by the author. xxvii + 156pp. 7⅞ x 10¾. 20011-6 Paperbound $3.50

1800 WOODCUTS BY THOMAS BEWICK AND HIS SCHOOL. This is the largest collection of first-rate pictorial woodcuts in print—an indispensable part of the working library of every commercial artist, art director, production designer, packaging artist, craftsman, manufacturer, librarian, art collector, and artist. And best of all, when you buy your copy of Bewick, you buy the rights to reproduce individual illustrations—no permission needed, no acknowledgments, no clearance fees! Classified index. Bibliography and sources. xiv + 246pp. 9 x 12.

20766-8 Paperbound $4.00

THE SCRIPT LETTER, Tommy Thompson. Prepared by a noted authority, this is a thorough, straightforward course of instruction with advice on virtually every facet of the art of script lettering. Also a brief history of lettering with examples from early copy books and illustrations from present day advertising and packaging. Copiously illustrated. Bibliography. 128pp. 6½ x 9⅛.

21311-0 Paperbound $1.25

Dover Books on Art

THE COMPLETE BOOK OF SILK SCREEN PRINTING PRO-DUCTION, J. I. Biegeleisen. Here is a clear and complete picture of every aspect of silk screen technique and press operation—from individually operated manual presses to modern automatic ones. Unsurpassed as a guidebook for setting up shop, making shop operation more efficient, finding out about latest methods and equipment; or as a textbook for use in teaching, studying, or learning all aspects of the profession. 124 figures. Index. Bibliography. List of Supply Sources. xi + 253pp. 5⅜ x 8½.
21100-2 Paperbound $2.75

A HISTORY OF COSTUME, Carl Köhler. The most reliable and authentic account of the development of dress from ancient times through the 19th century. Based on actual pieces of clothing that have survived, using paintihgs, statues and other reproductions only where originals no longer exist. Hundreds of illustrations, including detailed patterns for many articles. Highly useful for theatre and movie directors, fashion designers, illustrators, teachers. Edited and augmented by Emma von Sichart. Translated by Alexander K. Dallas. 594 illustrations. 464pp. 5⅛ x 7⅛.
21030-8 Paperbound $3.00

CHINESE HOUSEHOLD FURNITURE, G. N. Kates. A summary of virtually everything that is known about authentic Chinese furniture before it was contaminated by the influence of the West. The text covers history of styles, materials used, principles of design and craftsmanship, and furniture arrangement—all fully illustrated. xiii + 190pp. 5⅝ x 8½.
20958-X Paperbound $1.75

THE COMPLETE WOODCUTS OF ALBRECHT DURER, edited by Dr. Willi Kurth. Albrecht Dürer was a master in various media, but it was in woodcut design that his creative genius reached its highest expression. Here are all of his extant woodcuts, a collection of over 300 great works, many of which are not available elsewhere. An indispensable work for the art historian and critic and all art lovers. 346 plates. Index. 285pp. 8½ x 12¼.
21097-9 Paperbound $3.00

Dover publishes books on commercial art, art history, crafts, design, art classics; also books on music, literature, science, mathematics, puzzles and entertainments, chess, engineering, biology, philosophy, psychology, languages, history, and other fields. For free circulars write to Dept. DA, Dover Publications, Inc., 180 Varick St., New York, N.Y. 10014.